VOID

by

Alla Vilnyanskaya

With Translations of Poems by Anastasia Afanas'eva

Void

Copyright © 2021 Alla Vilnyanskaya

"Hedgehog," "Untitled," & "Untitled" Copyright © Anastasia Afanas'eva, used with permission. Translations from Russian by Alla Vilnyanskaya

All rights reserved.

No part of this publication may be reproduced, distributed, or transmitted in any form or by any means, including photocopying, recording, or other electronic or mechanical methods, without the prior written permission of the publisher, except in brief quotations embodied in critical reviews, citations, and literary journals for noncommercial uses permitted by copyright law.

ISBN-13: 978-1-7345158-8-6

Cover artwork by Alla Vilnyanskaya

Printed in the U.S.A.

For more titles and inquiries, please visit:

www.thirtywestph.com

In memory of Jesse Kushner (1979-2004)
& Iegudes Riskin (1916-2010)

What's Inside

#2666	10
Scene	11
Not a Flood, but What's Left After	12
Lost Park	14
Morning	16
After Primo Levi	18
September 28, 2012	19
Mara	22
Puma	23
Statue	24
Cinderella: Master Class, Practicing on the Violin	26
Pine	27
As I Sit by My Lover's Bed	28
Observation Deck	29
Letter	30
I Wish I Knew You	31
Jelly Bean	32
Tennis Ball	33
Encounter	37
Anniversary Gift	40
Grave	42
Shadow	43
It Was Always the Same	44
Sandbox	45
Cartoon	49
Pink	50
Red	51
Albatross	52

Thief	53
Parade	54
Pikuach Nefesh	55
Parlor	57
An Elegy for Herb	58
Not Finding the Right Word at the Kiosk	59
Mulch, Grass, Green!	60
Circus	61
Homerun	62
Mother of Pearl	64
Homebound	65
Gray	66
Rubble	67
Some Notes on Witchcraft	68
Hut on Chicken Legs	69
Sharon Stone	70
Anti-Love Poem	71
On Lenin's Mausoleum and Love	72
After Donald Justice	73
Lot's Wife	74
Demeter	75
Mythology	76
S/hell	77
Appendix	78
Hedgehog	82
Untitled	86
Untitled	89
Previous Publications	91
Notes	92
About the Author	93

A big thanks to my professors at Miami University and Columbia University for helping me to put together this manuscript. A special thank you to Richard Howard who edited many of these poems.

VOID

#2666

When you spend a majority of time
reading about senseless murder
is this how it feels:
first surprised
then intrigued?

Finally, droning through the pages
you begin to question the intentions
of the author

The victim is choked
her hyoid bone broken
5ft seven, hair: blond eyes: hazel
checkered skirt rolled above the knees

in her rectum they find semen
a numb sensation takes over
Nothing, at the bottom of evil

Scene

In my dream
there was a body
several bodies
one body with a tag on the feet
It was cold
someone was teaching me how to place a tag
on the body.

They said to place it on the first big toe
Your father is at the doctor's office
they said he will be back tomorrow
Daddy, where are you? I am scared to call

There is a man asleep perpetually on our floor
they programmed me a lot of bad things
I could write a book, but not like Derrida

Growing up as a male is harder
Separating the girl in the room from the man
who is pointing the gun to her head
the girl in the room
with the gun pointed at her head is screaming
I am having trouble discerning the victim
from the assassin because
it's all part of the same shot

Not a Flood, but What's Left After

I.

A train crashed, leaving
us like antique dolls
draped over our seats.
I looked at their faces
to see if one of them was me.
Had I survived?
I couldn't face myself
I couldn't face my mom
two visitors on boats, old women
beside the train station.
Dried apricots and sunflower
seeds. I was afraid
none would taste good.

II.

Small pebbles in the water
beating against rocks—
I brush my teeth and spit
out blood. Insidious
penetrating, people want,
want something. I open
my mouth, and say "no."

III.

I hang my hopes in front of you, on a clothing line.
The wind blows them down.

IV.

In Lviv, two stores
only for buttons. They ask me to
pay for each cup of tea.
I sit sipping staring at
the newlywed couples
making their way
through the streets.

V.

At night the restaurant
next to our hotel is covered
with a clear tarp. Topless
girl on the stage.

VI.

This city was made under
water, then drained.
In front of the opera house
a fountain.

VII.

We stack words. For dinner
I eat cement. You try to pick it
from my gums with a bent paperclip.

Lost Park

It's time to come clean I said
I was only partially kidding about the voodoo doll
And in that dream I had,
I am pretty sure that we were holding hands

That night I stormed out on the road at three am
I think it was because I had grown sick
With promises made by men
Nearly a decade younger, than I am beginning to understand
The things you find most endearing about me
Aren't the ones I was hoping you would latch on to
Like that time I said
That a person's soul
Is located inside their brain
And that my ex, had no brain
You should have understood
That my brain, that my head
Literarily split
in two

At some point, I was told
That he would never come back
Though criminals often return
To the scene of the crime

There is nothing left of you
But bone and sun
There is nothing left of me
Except for cartilage

That day you let me
fall from the Brooklyn Bridge
You thought you would never see me again
in fact, your greatest fear is that we would have anything in common

In your sleep
you are saying
I don't want to be you
my father
how men will torture you

My bra
Slapped me in the face
Stop touching yourself

Are you waiting for me to be different?
Braver?
You want me to appear like myself again?
What devil-like creature would I have to become
To bend you over again

Forgetting
Games
Forgetting
To come home at night

Morning

This year we eat only *PowerBars*
since I can't seem to stuff anything else
down my esophagus
I feel good when I wake at the crack of dawn

There are no roosters here
no cock-a-doodle-doo,
but there are crickets, and fireflies
the hum-drum of people's cars at night

If you really want to know the truth
here is what I think
you are not my mother

I think my mother perished
for women like you
in the tumults
of her own sorrow

a sparrow smashing its beak
against glass
behind which the devil

masked his physiognomy
Calculating probability
to get back to you

I would have to move
faster than the speed of light,
which means I would have to be dead

If there is no life after this
I must slow down
I must act myself, as a God.

We're sitting in a room filled with people
neither of us know that well
we're speaking of economics, politics,
and neoliberalism.

You look thinner than before,
but your eyes look like a cleaner, healthier
blue than I remember
which means that the angels
of modern medicine
have smiled upon you
You speak of how the capitalist regime has exploited your body and I am not sure that I believe you.

Last week when I was at Maya's house Maya said, "God suck me please," to her fiancée

God drown me in song.

After Primo Levi

It is not hot, nor cold, nor is there a wire to touch
There is only a slight wind

I picture a hearse driven through the streets of Turin.
You are no deader, now, than you were before
you decided to take your own life.

Only the shell of your body remains visible.
In a casket, carried through the streets
I wonder if there was a malignant God

When someone inadvertently murdered you
who lit the proverbial match
to cross a street at the red light

Led by a fictitious God, the radiation of a soul
The USSR, a stupid, malignant force
negligent in its wake as the forces of nature.

September 28, 2012

Today, everything smelled like musk
the man who cut locks of my hair
couldn't handle his comb.
On the way home
I was hit by a car
they said it was an accident.

HOMERUN

Mara

It's okay to not want to participate
in that pivotal moment, a global economy

of hills. Listen to my dream. Last night I am in the park
there is a dog, desperately needs walking.

A frog, plastic inside an aquarium, and a living one
in a jar, I can't tell the living from the plastic one when I find them.

The water is dirty like a swamp, which I would think
would be perfect for a frog *I would think*

It has been too long the game is no longer
about winning, the goal

is not winning; a battle with yourself, your own body
your addiction. Wife, grandmother who weeps.

But she cries even after she is gone, and I wonder if there
is a heaven in infidelity, or perhaps they still like to blame.

Some biblical scholars dictate: rape is something that woman
deserves to be punished for

Last summer I kept saying about my mom, that she killed
my grandfather over an item of clothing she desperately

needed and couldn't have in a fit of entitlement. My arm hurt
and I could kind of see it happening
all over again

Puma

27 letters in the alphabet
can I have a cigarette
the curtains
red is the color of love

I can't breathe, it's too late
the paper is white
it's a good laugh

I can't breathe it's too late
27 letters in the alphabet
can I have a cigarette
the paper is white

Statue

I.

Somewhere, in some part of
the   heavens   in   the   soil
someone   will   love   you   and
is waiting   not   me

One day   when   I come to
my father's   house   I see an
icon of   the Virgin   Mary
On   the   white dresser

II.

White Wormswrapped
round your   torso   drink
sorrow   slowly   and

let   them   take   you
from   me

III.

Anything   that's
alive is   capable
of love   your
Houseplant   died
right after.   V-day

IV.

I watch   the snow
change   to rain then
to sleet   a   car
swipesthepuddleat my
feet

V.

My father calls,
who is this
Eto ti?

Cinderella: Master Class, Practicing on the Violin

It takes special skill
to discern
that almost anything
may be ruined.

My mother plays her piano,
beats her knuckles against the black and white
keys, welds sounds together
fingers thick; nails painted crimson

Not the typical hands of a concert pianist.
Above her, depicted a young woman in Victorian dress.
The instrument, serving as her accessory; her captive.
Who unhinged the gates, through which
her carriage was set to arrive?

Pine

Heartwood rusts
between needles
and posts
rubbed hands
inhabit the
cold

As I Sit by My Lover's Bed

And let out nonsensical phrases
I must stick with men

Who won't shovel the snow
men with aspirations towards abstraction
higher than the twin towers

Observation Deck

If there is one thing that we can agree upon
it is the body

Standing on the rooftop
of one of Philadelphia's largest observation decks
I see only blue
Blue his eyes
blue the sky
Blue my veins

Do you remember how much fun we had
on the dog beach?

How they were all splashing and drowning

Standing atop of one of Philadelphia's largest observation decks
we see only blue
blue the sky
blue his heart
blue my veins
if there is one thing that we can agree upon
it is the body
here, take my hand

I've erased more than half of the poem to create enough space for you

Letter

While you were away
they named me after
one of the vilest women in history
and told me to tell you
that I will take my own life

But I do not dream of such a thing
I only want to know if you are alright, my love
Meanwhile, I really do feel
a stabbing pain in the center of my loins.

I have only had this feeling once when I was twenty-eight.
But as of late I feel it almost all of the time.

Nobody here writes digital poems.
They only speak of the Greeks and of love
in all of its possible versions.

And you will be happy to know
I have read almost all of the poetical works
of Paul Celan.

I Wish I Knew You

You have the prettiest gloves
you have the prettiest gloves
I can't breathe it's too late
stripes and stars

*

You have the prettiest gloves
it's a good laugh
at the train station

*

Twenty-seven letters in the alphabet
can I have a cigarette
the curtains
red is the color of love

*

I can't breathe, it's too late
the paper is white
it's a good laugh

Jelly Bean

It's like that game
sizing up the vessel
trying to ascertain
how many jelly beans
are in a jar

No one asks about
the color, texture, flavor

Tennis Ball

I.

Jaya had driven her car and suffered a massive concussion
"How many times have you tried to commit suicide?"

Sepia
When I was five my parents showed me a violent program on television. It was a show called *TiTi Peshe Shaloe* about a beautiful young woman with brown hair who was addicted to heroin. She fell in love with a cop. At some point, there was a madwoman in the attic of her husband's house. They succeeded in locking her there, while her husband moved on and led another life completely.

My husband, my ex-boyfriend, white dress, attic. *You can't just let yourself go like this.* I was locked in a basement and forced to take the blame for isolating myself. Women's emotions are fraudulent.

II.

When I was five, I told my grandmother that I wanted to jump off of the balcony. I was aiming for the one in the living room with all the glass, the large table, and the TV.

About Ira, they said he is a *podonok*, but I think he is worse. A *podonok* is still human. In March of 2014, I got into my car. I started to drive and thought I would definitely get into some kind of wreck.

I wanted to call him. I called his job, nobody answered; maybe they didn't receive the call.

I couldn't leave a message. It gave him some kind of satisfaction. The idiot was a big fan of *Black Swan*.

Maybe I did, or maybe I was past the point of attempting suicide. The idea that suicide would bring peace was remote.

They keep making me reincarnate.

III.

Don't give it a name

It feels like people these days are less scared of death
then they are of rejection
everyone wants to play doctor
Play soldier
play with fire

"What about me? The dog says, "I don't have a presence?"
"I loved you and was abandoned by my surrogate parents"
and here I am getting frostbite. Yes, you were led against and
maybe even away from me, but did you have no free will?"

Who am I? Am I the dog here, or the Indian Princess who threw
herself into a fire?

IV.

Ft. Lauderdale 2011

After my grandmother died
there was a moth infestation
in my apartment

Little worms somehow cocooned in every crevice
inside of the popcorn ceiling
we tried to beat them off with a broom
But they kept coming back

*

Fort Lauderdale—
I saw about 12 crows
they landed on our balcony
Two birds fighting
on the bench, one, female pecking
screaming and
real, or imagined
I saw a dragonfly
imprinted in the sand

V.

My father, walking with a cane
his mouth crooked
contorted from shingles

You can't keep beating a hearse—
a dead door bolt lock

He said he was like my father
that he didn't care about me
just like him
Three wives
one barely out of prison
one deemed mentally insane
Another with portraits of her daughter
all over her grand piano

VI.

Sapphire

My parents and I went to Disney world
my father took many pictures of me at the *Epcot Center*
While we were waiting, I saw a man standing in line
waiting for his girlfriend
He turned around and held out his hand
I sat down and refused to move
"He's not going to hurt you
What's wrong? Let's keep going,"

Milon had a friend who had a reputation

In a canopy bed
with black metal pieces
protruding under the mesh net
One day, blue eyes will kill you
I arrive home
one day too late
Barry draped over my shoulder
like a scarf; dead animal who knew, or begged, or pined
for his life

in the end
dead animal
voice over my mother's home
Sasha weeping and weeping:
Her hip torn off by a piece of metal.

Aziza like a ripe fruit
lives up to her name

How easily people forget
and live out self-fulfilling prophecies.

Encounter

A boy bounces
a tennis ball in the street
he sees a car
turning

TENNIS BALL

Anniversary Gift

I mean it's like he is happy for me
He just loves me, it
overpowers everything. Even his sense
of himself as male
who is generally afraid of intimacy.

He pretends that I am a beast.
He dreams about tying me up.
He carries a lock of my pubic hair in his wallet.

Some days, he doesn't shave.
He pulls his hair follicles out
in front of a foggy mirror.
Sleeping alone
next to some new girl.
He doesn't know her
care to know her, because

a small troll, in a red hat
has made all his decisions—
while on a plane to Alaska
he grew fond of glaciers.

I was dumb.
I never looked him up until it was too late.

He tried to confuse me.
There was no hope.
I tried.
I am supposed to be happy.

You shouldn't have said five years.
You should have said tomorrow, or fifty.
Try saying tomorrow.

Grave

Describe a time when you feel that you have acted very bravely, with great courage.
Describe a time in your life when you feel that you could have shown a bit more courage or strength.
Describe yourself in five words, or less.
Describe yourself in one sentence.
What would you say is your relationship with your family?
Describe the last time that you felt unsafe.
Have you ever been in love?
Describe a time when you were hurt by someone you loved very much.
Describe the level of pain that you are feeling right now from one to five.
What is your pain on a scale from 1 - 10?

Shadow

He never fell in love
with the girl
only her shadow
he followed
biting, kicking, licking

After she passed away
he curled up
in the spot
where they had first met

The snow fell
but, he never came

It Was Always the Same

in a small room
don't eat me
let's play cards

How often do you have dreams that you are trapped?
He is always in the room
playing
Queen of hearts

"Books know
what your dreams mean"

Is there blood?
"No"
Good.

Sandbox

A Poetry Play

The playground is empty aside from two small children (age unknown) *toying in the sandbox. The sun shines down upon them in an awkward slant.*

Girl: Can I please have the sand bucket?
(Echo): Mogu ya imet' vedro, pozhaluysta?
Translator: Am I allowed to have the bucket, please?

(Boy *sits in silence.*)
(Girl *gives* Boy *a strange look.*)
(Boy *is oblivious.*)
(Girl *molds sand in front of her into a small heap.*)

Boy: What's that?
(Echo): Chto eto takoye?
Translator: What is this?
Girl: Can I have the sand bucket?
(Echo): Mogu ya vzyat' vedro s peskom?
Translator: Am I allowed to take the bucket full of sand?
Boy: Sure
(Echo): Konechno
Translator: Of course, without reserve.

(Girl *tears bucket from* Boy's *hands and begins to use it as a shovel.*)

Boy: You might want to take this! (*Gives* Girl *the shovel.*)
(Echo): Mozhet byt' vy budete ispol'zovat' etu veshch'?

Translator: Maybe you will use this thing?
Girl: I don't need it.
(Echo): Mne ne nuzhno eto.
Translator: Maybe you will use this thing?
Girl: I don't need it.

(Echo): Mne ne nuzhno eto.
Translator: I am not in need of this thing.
Boy: OK.
(Echo): Khorosho.
Translator: Good.
Girl: Where is your mom?
(Echo): Gde tvoya mama?
Translator: Where is the mom that belongs to you?
Boy: Somewhere, I don't know, she will arrive here.
Girl: My father will pick me up.
(Echo): Moy otets sobirayetsa otvezti menya domoy.
Translator: My father will take me home.
Boy: I don't have a father
(Echo): U menya net ottsa
Translator: I don't have any father.

Girl: Why not?
(Echo): Pochemu?
Translator: (*accusatory*) Why?
Boy: Can you give me back the bucket?

(Girl *hands bucket over to the* Boy. Boy *starts to fill it with sand; becomes distracted.* Girl *stares at* Boy *with curiosity.*)

Boy: What?
Girl: Nothing
(Echo): Nichego takogo.
Translator: Not a fig.

(*Another* Boy *enters the scene, his mother has just dropped him off at the playground, saying she will be back in a half an hour.*)

Boy 2: Hello, my name is Alex, can I play with you?
(Echo): Zdravstvuyte, menya zovut Aleks, ya mogu poigrat' svami?

Translator: Hello, I am called Alex, am I allowed to play with you?
Girl: Of course

(Boy 2 *shrugs and begins vehemently to work in the sandbox, in minutes constructing what looks like a sculpture of a tortoise.*)

Girl: Wow, how did you do that?
(Echo): Kak ty eto delayesh'?
Translator: How did you make this?
Boy 2: Look, this is what you do.

(Boy 2 *begins to show* Girl *how to build tortoise.*)

(Echo): Smotri, vot kak eto dolzhno byt' sdelano.
Translator: Look, this is how you must do it.

(*While* Boy 2 *is busy showing* Girl *how to build an identical tortoise out of sand,* Boy 1 *kicks over his new creation.*)

Girl: Hey!
Boy 2: Why did you do that?
(Echo): Pochemu ty eto delayesh?
Translator: Why are you doing this?

(Boy 1 *remains silent.*)
(Boy 2 *moves to the opposite end of the sandbox.*)

Boy 1: Let him play by himself!

(Girl *looks distraught.*)

Boy 2: Well I better get going. (*Walks off.*)
(Echo): Lutshi uyti seychas
Translator: I think it's time to go.

Boy 1: Retard!
(Echo): Durak!
Translator: Fool!

(Girl's Father *comes to pick her up from the playground.*)

Father: And who is this? Would you like to introduce me to your new friend?
Girl: This is Alex.
(Echo): Eto Aleks.
Translator: This is Alex.
Father: It's very nice to meet you, Alex.
(Echo): Ochen' priyatno poznakomit'sya s toboy Alex.

(Girl *looks away.*)

Father: Are you ready to go?
(Echo): Poydem vmeste?
Translator: Let's go.

(Girl *stands up and walks off with her father.*)
(Boy 1 *continues to play by himself.*)

THE END

Cartoon

My father makes square-shaped airplanes
from farmer's cheese
puts a cold towel on my arm
soothing my bee stings
points to a truck:

If you don't eat
Crocodile Genya
will steal you.

Pink

*

When I started seeing him I had no trouble sleeping. No trouble with boundaries. I had trouble. A girl goes to work, comes home, and prepares dinner. Somebody sees her, wants her and wants himself inside of her. It happens. She makes it happen. Here is the confusion. Not everyone has learned enough. I was told to keep my nose clean. I should have made myself clearer when I said I am not vouching for you nor betting against you under any circumstances. Do not blame the woman; nor child.

*

I picture you nude, rose pink. You fit inside me. You are so low I bet you spoke about my underwear with your new girlfriend. It seems we live in a place where everything is short-lived. Where people are only capable of short memories. This also pertains to those whom we love.

*

I said no and it sounded like "Yes. Yes. Yes. Please take me, right here. In fact, I would prefer it if we didn't wear any clothing." There is a certain way that after a rape the sound of a woman's voice changes. She becomes an angel. She hears voices and sees colors he would never have otherwise seen.

Red

May I have a glass of water?

We don't pick our parents
another childhood

Wanting to be
another person

A vase doesn't ask for
the clay it is made of

A flower blossoms

feigns distance

A boom box in a desert
Dali painting all

Bewilderment
This is a dandelion

Albatross

His fingers fat like mosquitos
His face gold
as the nape of an albatross
His belly full

I saw a man washing strawberries outside of my home today
He was washing them in a zinc tub. I went to lick the
triangular puffs.

The lovers were then taken aboard a ship
and never heard from again

That story.

Thief

He sees her
Live a vision
Steals her
Like a jewel
Lulls her
Like a baby
Unwraps her
Like a chocolate
Uses her like a
Sheet
Breaks her
Like a twig
buries her

Parade

These days have marched past me like troops
trampling on my firstborn
and me running beside them
a gypsy after her caravan

Pikuach Nefesh

—and the light snuffed from their eyes

Any animal
which chews
on its
own cud
and has
a Cloven Hoof is
clean. Break
the rules
when a
human life
is at
stake.
To precise
depth severing
both Carotid
Arteries both
Jugular Veins
Both Vagus Nerves.
The Trachea
and the
Esophagus, no
higher than
the Epiglottis
and no
lower than
where cilia
begin inside
the trachea
the animal
bleeding to
death. Animals
That only
chew cud,

or only
have cloven

hooves are
unclean. An
insect born
inside a
fruit may
be eaten
if it
has never
crawled on
the ground.
The same
principles never
apply to
an animal
that has
not been
checked for
disease. Allocate
the fat
to God.
Strict guidelines
require that
you kill
with a single
cut.

Parlor

Love is easily seen from the balcony
with the sad vision of a phantom

I am looking for meaning in letters
in the gallantry of the last dance

Women gather to speak of the next day
Cold wind battles against the sky
while nature rests indifferently

The night is young and time goes quickly
I am crawling out of my skin
People are distracting me

I've gotten what I wanted
and no longer want what I have

The woman is gone because
she has found someone else

An Elegy for Herb

As often happens with illness
you become a person buried
inside the tomb of your body

Just a few months ago
you were more like a tree branch
dry, black.
But now I see the sky has once again
Opened inside your pupils

I want to tear
your soul
out of its lizard-like shell.

Not Finding the Right Word at the Kiosk

If the poem is smarter than you by far
I shall stand beside it always
like a dog beside a trophy not even earned
I shall write backward
That is, I shall write from right to left
from the back of the book to the cover
Language that makes its way inside the body
Like intravenous fluid, administered before an MRI,
melancholy

Madame, if I may be so bold, you're giving yourself too much credit and in all the wrong ways.

Obsession: the action, or state of being forced to do something
Constraint: an irresistible urge to behave in a certain way

Mulch, Grass, Green!

My fondest memory, drawn from a picture
running around with mom and dad
proudly placing a pine cone in front of the camera
If only I hadn't fallen off of my bike

Circus

The water was muck green
looking inside it was like
looking into the eyes of a person
whom you don't really trust.

The cold wind numbed my fingers.
How many park benches have I sat on?
Shall we make this a tradition?

The boat dock was raised up
against the metal cage, propelling
from what looked like a bungee cord
strung up with yellow tubes.

Leaves flew across the pavement.
Something screeched. I heard
the cry of cantankerous birds.

The sky looked as if
someone had drawn clouds in
with pastel.

We walked a lot. I was silent.
Best not to think when you are freezing
your paws off.

Homerun

I.

Do you recall playing baseball
white stripes
upon trampled grass
sand colored dirt

where you're the kind of player
who missed all the shots
tagged before you hit home

did you wait reticently
on the metal slabs
scorching from sun
talking with friends
find comfort in the feel of the leather glove,
or have a crush on a guy who was
perpetually throwing the ball

II.

Telegram

Put together (carefully)
the letter was signed—

a small worm crawling
out of the corner I had
yet to secure shut
I misspelled the word
oh "dear"
too much dumb luck

III.

Dedication

I've always hated
plastic flowers,
but as I grow older
I realize that one
does not always
have the time
or patience
to sustain
a living thing

I have these white carnations
that my mother gave me
peeking out of
the too tall vase
they are lined with

Gold trim on
the petals, green
stems, hidden in
the crystal designs

Mother of Pearl

I was living in a room
sleeping in a bed
enclosed in barbed wire

A wire
out of which
I should have been extracted
You were the girl
he fell in love with

My father's father fled Ukraine
during the Nazi occupation of Kharkov
leaving his wife and son

We ate potato peels
And crawled over severed limbs

You were the girl my father fell in love with
and cried for on a train
going from nowhere, to elsewhere.

Homebound

I understand now, my dear
how you not wanting me to be alone
was a reflection of how alone you felt
and how my distress at this
was reflected in being unable to accept your company

In one year I have aged a hundred
by placing cigarettes in my mouth, like paper drums.
Last night, drifting in sleep
I saw his face again.

My grandfather's death
before the cemetery.
Stones resemble
Halloween decorations.

The miracle of my grandmother sitting
for years before her time came
cutting out newspaper articles to send to us;
planning her funeral.

Gray

You may live through a war
or wait too long
at the grocery store
checkout line

Rubble

If you are still unashamed of your lifestyle
concrete troubles the debris
your tongue a white mesh
my smile stretched thin
a mess, a new one—
flesh fibers in the rubble

Some Notes on Witchcraft

My copy
of *The Book of Frank*
by the man himself
it opens up with the lines

This book is dedicated
to all poets everywhere
which upon first glance
makes me all warm
and fuzzy inside

Hut on Chicken Legs

Our house had no rules
breadcrumbs on the bed
makeup on the stove

you ask that I read by a lamp
You spill kerosene on the floor

Sharon Stone

So it's just me and Sharon Stone
sitting in the vestibule
we both hit our heads
and lost our men
What goes up must come down
right?

Anti-Love Poem

you are a desk-lamp
a kind of disease—
random lottery ticket
the short straw I drew
unwittingly not ever
realizing what it could bring

On Lenin's Mausoleum and Love

Not every glance is capable of conveying
all things at once: love, anger, frustration.

I remember your mother's house;
the inside of a ship.

I know you thought things would be alright
turning to sand,
all of it coming down.

In "Love Letter to a Stranger"
you're always you and I'm always me.

A body you'll do anything to preserve.

After Donald Justice

Is it snowing out?
Is it snowing in?
Are you a spectacle?
Are you a harpsichord?
Are you an oasis?
What do you do in your free time?
Are you a river?
What do you bring with you when you travel?
What is your native tongue?
What is your favorite flower?
Do you feel apologetic?
Will you be atoning for your sins?
Is this your blanket?
Are you a Libra?
Are you a song of peaches?
Could you please remove your spectacles?
Is this a celebration?
Is this a teardrop, or a drop of rain?
Is there a word for sepal in your language?

Lot's Wife

My dear
I've left the door
Ajar, but without me
you may not return

Demeter

If you were to name one of your children
after a play by Shakespeare
would you insist the name mimic the sound
of a beating drum

Bassianus, Saturninus?
Or, would you shoot for something more delicate?
Perhaps you would attempt to mimic the hum of a woman
smearing lipstick onto her mouth
or placing the finishing touches on her new car
or maybe you would ask for something a little more
saccharine—

Like, the ringing of a thousand bells,

Or the smell of a particular flower.

Mythology

And if you asked me today
What happened between us
Why we split
I would tell you
That daemons came
And stole me from your bed
And after they took me away
They surrounded you

S/hell

When you crawl naked
sometimes into a
brighter bigger space
and sometimes into a small dark hole
that you are afraid to leave again
for fear of dying

Appendix

```
I      WANT      SOMEONE    TO      SEW ME UP
I WANT           SOMEONE TO SEW ME UP
I WANT           SOMEONE         TO SEW ME UP

I WANT SOMEONE          TO SEW ME UP
I WANT SOMEONE TO SEW ME UP
I WANT SOMEONE          TO SEW ME UP

I WANT      SOMEONE TO SEW ME UP
IWANT SOMEONE              TO SEW ME UP
```

TRANSLAT-
IONS

Poems by Anastasia Afanas'eva

Hedgehog

1.

Look what is happening on the terrain
of the earth. There is nothing in existence,
only a sieve anything smaller than its holes
falls into the abyss

And that which is larger—lies
shining, under some bright bush
at night, a lost phone

No one is there to pick up.

2.

The void grows and grows,
and stands at full height
all of its glass height,
simple as the word "yes."

It grows like a flood
impossible to conduct
as if after killing a hedgehog
the killer is followed by its shadow
all of his life.

3.

Who fell inside the void?
Who can discern?
I would make a speech,
but there is nothing left to do,
but run a long time ago
here and onboard with us.

He who will find deep waters here
will surely drown.
He does not believe what he is told
There is not a drop around, only sand

In a city sink,
he learns the fate of the river.

4.

The oblivion grows and grows
as large as pink-skinned fruit.
He cannot say where he is from
and who he is and why.

I afflict his smooth skin with my touch,
and later spit straight into his forehead.

The spit flows down his forehead
as if it were skidding on ice,
these passions for him are out of place.
His face is deprived of flaws.
He is not able to mourn, nor laugh.

Here, he has dried out,
and all that is left is more shine.
·He is smooth, white, and has so much gloss
that I begin to suspect that he is flat,
and this is what brings him joy.
In a three-dimensional world,
he knows neither volume nor depth.

5.

Look what is happening:
for those who were helplessly drowning
the earth opened its black chasm.

About them, we cannot speak,
for they are completed.
And behind them,
dropping to the bottom, goes the praise.

6.

Look how your mound has grown in,
where there was a creek,
now there is moss.
where there is a stream—there is a gap,
the gap reliably patches itself with grass.

Your places release that,
which make them yours
and they become nothing
more than places.

See how life outlives us all,
the life that you carried; a nail inside
flies like a spear at impossible heights,
losing its weight in flight.

Your skin tightens
for this is how you are made.
Look how everything has healed,
and that which towered from every side,
like a gigantic ocean,
in the white sink murmurs,
and when you are irritated by the splash
you turn the faucet off.

7.

Look at what is happening on the earth:

It has become smooth,
grown in with pavement like grass
and the roads with a new black
highlight their whiteness.

And the air, gigantic inside of you
pierces all of the openings,
along your spine, the void is hammered in
with a glass nail.

It is impossible to return
to a place where there is nothing left
to return to someone who is no longer there.
You can't call this person, and in any case
there is no one to reach.

Do not turn back to the roads
which you have already passed,
you walk on the past
as if on a hedgehog.

And another water is calling.

Untitled

***

The air is cut in two by the morning sun.

To left—March, and to the right,
in the shadow—winter.

Into the shade crawls a dark blue,
gray, blue-black, frosty wind the
crunch crawls into the shadow,
untouched snow with traces of dog prints
the desperate stance under a winter sky,
hunt for white uncatchable butterflies
the cold of hands, not belonging and rootless
standing in the dark,
as if you had turned your back to God,
a ravine in front of your eyes
other signs of winter—
retreating into the shade.

A girl in a red jacket goes out into the sun,
her dog, meeting a passerby in an
orange down jacket, red-headed boy, desperate
bravery, happy leap into suspense
of the unknown, other signs of prosperity,
strong, like birth, and visible, like sun
growing in March, because life grows
always in places where there is light.

So I thought about what would happen
if everything became clear if the boundaries
were marked, and the mixing was abolished
the mixing of the incompatible,
but still connected
in one.

How I wanted to fly, like a plane,
so that I could see from atop,
the whole godly grid—
the place of my small knot
in everything that has been weaved
so that I would know how many kilometers
of thread responded to each one of my
small movements.

How one person becomes the reason
for another's existence
how a small event is preceded
by something of significance
thereby becoming significant.

How two things form a third,
how they are transformed
and how they exist subsequently
in everything that follows;
how what follows cancels
that which precedes it,
while depending on it completely.

How he *(God)* places things
and meshes details.

I wanted to see what shape and contours
our collective lives have
if we looked upon them as an entirety,
and not from the small
vantage point of our own existence,
but from a fantastical airplane
like wheat fields from a satellite.

Oh, how I wanted, and in the natural
human inability

I, connected, I inseparable
felt:

I—am small,

I—am big.

Untitled

So many echoes surround us
It is impossible to discern a voice
To the left and to the right, an echo

As if it walked around in a circle
Itself reflecting
And everyone had long ago forgotten
The person who let out a cry

What word happened?
Did you call for help
Or praise the sky and the earth—

We will never recognize it
And we will never see.
Lost in the orbit of blind sound
Repetition of repetitions,
doubled without the double
We attach to the massive noise
our inarticulate whispers,
Cheers, shouts

The earth sounds with voices
The air is filled with voices

I stand up as straight as I can and close my eyes
I will stand quietly like the water and trees—
And in this helpless stance become stronger

To greet another silence
I will pour out with silence
I will be filled with that which
I encounter and we will become one
As if that voice that is impossible to hear
Unable to find, secret
Everything of utmost importance
I will tell you in silence
And what is not important will multiply;
be spoken by the echo

Previous Publications

"After Primo Levi" received Honorary Mention in *The Writer's Workshop of Asheville, NC* writing contest

"#2666" was published in the *On Barcelona Blog*

"Scene" was published in *ZO Magazine*

"Master Class: Cinderella Practicing Violin" & "On Lenin's Mausoleum and Love" were published in *Thick with Conviction*

"Letter" was published in *Boog City*

"Tennis Ball" was published in *Another New Calligraphy*

"Thief" was published in *Transient Literary Magazine*

"Gray" was published in *Gambling the Aisle*

"Lot's Wife" & "Parade" were published in *Schlag Magazine*

"Mother of Pearl" was published in *Zaum Magazine*

"An Elegy for Herb" was published in *Saint Ann's Review*

"Demeter" was published in *Ligeia Magazine*

"Appendix" was published in *45th Street Parallel*

"Pikuach Nefesh" was published in *Coffin Bell Journal*

"Parlor" was published in *Evocations Review*

'Lost Park" was published in *Chantarelle's Notebook* under the title, "Kaleidoscope"

Translations of "Hedgehog" was published by *Asymptote Blog*

Notes

1. The poem, "#2666," was written after Roberto Bolaño

2. The poem, "Albatross," was written after Joan Didion and Anne Sexton

3. The poem, "Parlor," was written after "Spleen" by Charles Baudelaire

4. The poem, "An Elegy for Herb," was written for Max Ritvo

5. The poem, "Homebound," was written after Iegudes Riskin, my Grandmother

6. The poem, "On Lenin's Mausoleum and Love," was written after Jenny Browne's "Love Letter to a Stranger."

About the Author

Alla Vilnyanskaya was born in Ukraine and raised in the U.S. She came to Philadelphia in 1989 with her parents. She holds an MA from Miami University and an MFA from Columbia University. Her work has been published in multiple online and print journals including *Zaum, Poetry International, Saint Ann's Review,* and *Boog City.* She is an alumna of The Home School and has won several teaching fellowships and other awards from Miami University and Columbia University.

About the Author in translation

Anastasia Afanas'eva was born in 1982. She graduated from the Medical University of Kharkov with a degree in psychiatry. She worked in her field at the Kharkov Psychiatric Hospital. Her poetry, prose, and criticism of contemporary poets have been published in numerous journals and anthologies including *Air*, *The New World*, *Vavilon*, and others. She is a translator of poetry from English and Ukrainian. Most recently she successfully translated the work of Ilya Kaminsky, *Musica Humana* (New York: Ayloros, 2012). She received a Laureate Prize from the journal *Word* in 2005, The Russian Award in 2006, a prize from *Literary X-Ray* in 2007, and a Shortlist Prize in *Debut* in 2003. Her work has been translated into English, Italian, Dutch, and Belorussian.

www.ingramcontent.com/pod-product-compliance
Lightning Source LLC
Chambersburg PA
CBHW020545080526
44583CB00013B/998